I'm not so Special!

I'm not so Special!

An ordinary girls journey into the extraordinary

Clare Luscombe

Dedication

To all who may learn about my journey and begin their own journey into the extraordinary.

Life is merely a journey to the heart. May you all find the strength to find your way home!

Acknowledgements

I would like to thank with all my heart:

My teacher and Mentor (for many lifetimes), Mike Way, without whom I would never have found my way.

My best friend Jess who has supported me during my journey (again!) and the lovely Linda who was there to pick up the pieces on many occasions!

Writer, author and amazing human, Zoe Owl, who has inspired me throughout.

My wonderful mum and dad who taught me resilience and how to be a good human!

And of course, my amazing husband Mike and beautiful daughter Karuna who are my world.

With all my love and gratitude.

Clare

Contents

Chapter One - The Early Years

So, life started very un-interestingly, with me being born to an average family, the second child of a family with a boisterous and 'needy' first child.

I was born underweight, undernourished and at death's door…. the doctors said because my mum was a heavy smoker (she wasn't, but her family were, and she spend most of her time with them… the joys of passive smoking!) her placenta had started to breakdown before I was ready to be born. So, there I was tiny, struggling for life with a bad case of reflux meaning that I couldn't keep anything down, I wasn't putting on weight but I survived.

I didn't have any ill health after those first few years. I was into sports and fitness and was generally your average youngest child, a little spoilt, a little bullied and left out by my older sister but average in every way! My mum worked part time to help pay the bills and my dad worked shifts. Life was ordinary!

And then things started to happen to the people around me. My nan died, which broke my mums heart (and everyone else's in her family). I was only seven so don't really remember a lot…but I do remember the aftermath. My mum's breakdown, my dad's tears, my sister moving school because of bullying and my grandad's suicide. This was all before my teenage years. Oh yes, and one of my favourite cousins dying at only 21.

Then life seemed to calm down a bit. I didn't get on overly well with my sister or mum at times and it seemed like it was me and my dad against the world. I didn't really feel like I fitted in anywhere and just kind of tried to 'fit in' as best I could. I had a pretty average school life, a bit of bullying, some fun, average grades. I just kept my head down and 'blended in'. I went to Uni as I really didn't know what else to do, getting in by the skin of my teeth from a fluke 'A' grade in a subject I didn't even like. My life was ordinary! I left Uni and started a career in fitness, jumping jobs as the wind took me, finally moving back home to decide what to do with life...I had no idea!

Field Note

So, why have I told you all this stuff....so you have a background to what life was like...my early years....my ordinaryness....my lack of anything extraordinary.

Chapter Two - What Happened!

I knew I liked health and fitness but that was about it and at the time you were either a fitness instructor or a PE teacher. So, I went back to Uni to do my teaching degree, again by the skin of my teeth... getting in after my third application!

Then things started to wrong for me. I got into a relationship with a boy/man I knew from school. I had always avoided him at school for some reason even though he had asked me out a lot... this time I changed my mind. He was good looking and seemed fun! It was a bad relationship which lasted too long, ending with a series of unwanted events including an abortion during teacher training and a broken heart for me.

I couldn't get to grips with some of the concepts in teacher training or why we taught the way we did and found out I was dyslexic, which made life even harder! Now anyone who has dyslexia will realise that it gets worse when you are stressed...reports, planning, schemes of work, meetings, target setting, essays and all the things that come with teacher training do not lead to a stress-free life!

I didn't want to do the course anymore, but everyone was telling me not to give up, I was doing so well, and my pride took over. I was going to finish the course and get a job in teaching... partially because one of my mentors told me I would be no good and failed me at every opportunity! I was determined to prove her and anyone else that doubted me wrong!

And so, I got a teaching job and started my career. It was fine at first and I quite liked it but then the school I was working at shut and I opted to take another job offered to me in a local school. I didn't fit in as well at this school and the ethos was different. I was used to working with troubled teens and this school was a highflying school. I started to feel depressed and that age-old itch to move jobs had come back but I was an adult, a teacher, I had to be responsible...so I stayed!

And then my nan got Alzheimer's and a long and painful road was ahead (my grandad had died a few years earlier with dementia, so I kind of knew what to expect). She didn't recognise us or speak to us, she sat in her own world somewhere far away from us. I went to see her just before she died, she did recognise me, but she was a shadow of her former self. I will never forget the guilt I felt because I couldn't see her before this as it was just too painful.

Field Note

A few wrong moves and it can all go a bit Pete Tong!

Chapter Three – Down Hill

And that was it, the start of my ill health…. always sick at holiday time, tired A LOT, chronic back ache….and worst of all stress and depression. It was an unhappy time for me…my energy was low, my vibration was low, I was low!

I got signed off work with stress and depression, visited the doctor numerous times about my bad back…to which one lovely doctor did actually tell me, it was stress related! Yes, my chronic back ache that had been getting worse for years was due to stress…even the western doctor that I saw told me that.

So, that was it, something had to change. But how…I was stuck!! I was earning good money……which I wouldn't be able to get anywhere else in the Westcountry. I had trained for 4 years to be here…. not to mention the other 8 years of on the job training to keep my knowledge and skills up. My mental health was shot, I had no confidence, no drive, no desire to do…well anything really, who would employ me anyway…? I did the only thing I could do…. I reduced my hours at work, lowered my monthly bills, cut spending and hoped for the best!

At this point I was married to an amazing man (Mike), who I am still married to now. He was my rock, my smile at the end of the day…he was my safe place (although I don't know how he put up with me, I was moody, grumpy, sad, I pushed him away, but he stayed!).

A year later (after 18 months of trying) we got pregnant with my daughter. Two months later Mike got hit by a car…. not your normal accident but thrown 15ft in the air from a push bike when a car failed to see him and ran straight into him. Luckily, he wasn't severely damaged, (in that he wasn't made disabled) but he went from being fun loving and up for anything to having neck problems, back problems, pain in both shoulders, both hips, both legs and could only walk a short distance before being in severe pain due to compression injuries. He couldn't lift our 2-month-old baby, he couldn't help me around the house, he couldn't play Rugby which he loved so much, and his mood sank.

So not only was I struggling to keep my head above water in a job I didn't want to do anymore, having had depression for almost six years and chronic back pain from stress… my rock, my husband who had kept me together for so long was broken!

A year into life like this, my husband was finally showing signs of emerging from his depression. I had done a remedial therapies course to try and help him as I knew his injuries would be ongoing due to my background in sports and health, plus it was a welcome escape from life. I always wanted to do a course in sports injuries…so I saw a bit of a silver lining. Mike had seen consultants and physio's, remedial therapists, healers and finally there was light at the end of the tunnel. Mike's pain was reducing, he could pick up his daughter, he started to smile again, and life was going to be ok!

And then, the news we had always dreaded...a problem with the flat! We were renting out our flat as we were unable to sell as there was no equity in it due to the recession and we couldn't afford to pay back the excess. It was the roof...an extra £3000 debt hit us just as we were starting to see light at the end of the tunnel. We were now facing bankruptcy as we couldn't afford the repair work to the leaky and damaged roof.

And then it hit me, my lowest point ever. I had used so much energy trying to fight depression and the pain in my back and help Mike, trying to keep things together....I had no energy left. I couldn't face getting out of bed, let alone going into work, my back was bad and it was radiating out into my hips. I could hardly walk a mile before crippling pain set in and I felt so bad as Mike was the one who got injured, the one who had a 'reason' to be broken!

So, by the ripe old age of 36, I had chronic back and hip pain, depression and was at the point of filing for bankruptcy! How had this happened...how had everything got so bad!

Field Note

Sometimes the worst things in life line us up for the best things in life!

Chapter Four - Rock Bottom

At this point life was a bit of a struggle. I lacked motivation, drive, the desire to do...well anything really! But I was a survivor, or so I told myself, I could get past this. I used to be happy, I used to have drive and desire and dreams...where had all my dreams gone. I didn't have any anymore!

You see I used to go with the flow, where my heart took me and think about the future later...but at some point, I had lost this. I had lost the desire to live in the moment, to do things spontaneously, to go where heart took me. It had gone, this connection to my heart and what I wanted to do had gone...it wasn't there anymore...nowhere to be seen!! How had this happened, how had I lost my 'spark'.

At the age of 18 I went to get a tattoo...it was small, the picture of a feather and the word 'spirit' in Chinese writing (although for all I knew it could have said anything) but that's what I wanted...to get it to remind me that I would never lose my spirit...that part of me that was fun loving, alive and ready for anything! But here I was, not even 20 years down the line with no clue how I lost that part of me, and no clue how to get it back!

I did what I said I would never do and went back to the doctor for the second time, a crying and blubbering mess in the hope that they would give

me something to help...and they did....
antidepressants and a month off work.

Field Note

Life without hopes and dreams is pretty bad.
Finding a 'spark' is all it takes!

Chapter Five – Finding a Spark!

During the month off work, I did what I knew I wasn't supposed to do…. I trawled through the job pages to find something that might spark something…anything in me, rather than stay in this pit of emptiness and lacklustre that I just couldn't seem to drag myself out of! And one job took my fancy, working with a young adult who had locked-in syndrome.

Could I get this job…I had no experience of practical support for someone in this position, but I did have theoretical knowledge…a lot of it from both personal experience and books. I had my remedial qualification, I had taught Health and Social Care to 'A' Level and I gave it a go. I wrote what I thought was complete rubbish at the time, given my depression and low mood I didn't think I had any skills or attributes that would help me to get the job. Something made me apply anyway in the hope that I may get an interview….and I did! I went for the interview, putting on my best 'I'm OK face' and blow me if I didn't get the job!

Now I was in a predicament…. they wanted me to start on Monday. I was still on sick leave…and I wasn't allowed to get a job on sick leave…and I had to give a full term's notice in work (that's 3 months!). So, I did the only thing I could, I scheduled an interview with the head to discuss things! I went into the office, tail between my legs, dreading what was going to happen. But, I got my head together, explained the situation and how I felt, tears and all and asked if I could be released from my contract that day. I knew it was a long shot and I was breaking my contract, but I asked anyway. The head looked at me, said, 'Well I wasn't expecting that...I had a job lined up for you in the behaviour unit'. (I was always really good with the troublesome kids, I just seemed to have the knack...but I had no idea the head had realised this about me!). Anyway, after a bit of thought she agreed to release me from my contract there and then. She could see I was broken and I just couldn't do it anymore and she had let me out of one part of my agony. Oh my god, I could do this, I could change my life!

Field Note

Things may not always be as bad as they seem, sometimes opening up and letting people know how you feel gets you what you need!

Chapter Six – The Shift

Two problems solved, Mike was feeling better and I no longer had a job I didn't want to be in. I had a nice new shiny job to entertain me for a while anyway and pay the bills while I sorted myself out. You know what they say, a change is just as good as a rest. I didn't stay in this job, but it gave me the breathing space and confidence to know that I was employable, and I did have skills (which at the time I didn't think I had). It also gave me the opportunity to really realise that actually my life wasn't that bad and to appreciate the simple pleasures I had in life, like being able to talk to people and having my own independence which the poor boy I was working didn't.

During this time I met up with an old friend from school. We had both had children around the same time and her youngest was a few months older than my little girl. I become friends with her husband who also went to the same school as us. They had been together a while and had finally decided to tie the knot. So, an invite to the hen do found its way to me (even though I spent more time talking to the husband at this point). It was nice to have been invited.

Four of us went away for a couple of nights to a lovely quiet retreat to get pampered and have some relaxation time. I had booked in for a Hot Stones Massage which I was really looking forward to and the moment came where I was lying down totally chilled having a massage and I got asked if I had a back problem. 'Yes', I said….'if you would like to have a go at fixing it be my guest!'. None of the health professionals I had seen at this point had been able to 'fix' my back so I didn't hold out a lot of hope! So, I let Mike (unbeknown to me at the time his nickname was 'Magic Mike') have a go at fixing my hips and back…and low and behold, 10 mins later I got off the bed like a new woman. It was instant, as soon as I got off the bed I could feel my back and hips were better, they felt more inline, like they hadn't felt in years! Plus, that heavy feeling I had been carrying around for so long had also gone…I felt light, and vibrant…and really happy!

Now at this point, I had quite a lot of knowledge about the body and how to fix it…after all I had done a Sports Science degree, taught Health and Social Care for years and done two Remedial Therapies Courses. And what he had done, was impossible…or so I thought! 'You can't do that I said to him' looking at him quizzically. 'Well, I can, and I just have' was his response!

Not one to be easily put off…I spent the rest of the weekend thinking about my hips and back being fixed and how by Western Medical standards it was impossible to do in 10 minutes. And, so began my love affair (albeit a little bit rocky) with the extraordinary… And all that 'Magic Mike' would later teach me!

Field Note

Just because you don't understand it, and no one told you it was possible.... doesn't mean it is impossible!

Chapter Seven – Releasing

And so...within the space of six months, I had changed my job, met up with old friends and my hips, back and mood had improved beyond recognition.... life was finally beginning to look up. But I just couldn't get what Mike (I call this Mike 'Magic Mike' to save confusion...I seemed to know a lot of Mike's!) had done out of my head. And randomly I seemed to be accumulating friends and acquaintances with a variety of health issues at a rapid pace. So, I did the only thing I could...I asked Magic Mike if he would come down and treat some of my friends to see if he could work his magic with them as well (and I did have a bit of an ulterior motive...I wanted to learn what he did!).

Magic Mike was down, I had so much to ask him...all of which went totally out of my head the moment I saw him and instead I broke down into tears...about...I don't even know what...I was just sad...about everything!

He didn't seem bothered and just got out some frankincense to fragrance the room and said, 'Let's take all that sorrow away' and gave me the most amazing hug! Now, three strange things happened here...I hadn't heard the word sorrow for a very long time, possibly since I had gone to Sunday School as a child, neither had I heard of the use of Frankincense since biblical times, all of which came flooding back to me there and then! I had also never experienced a hug that literally felt like

I had been transported home (I literally can't explain the feeling I had that day in a near strangers arms...and I was not a hugger. In fact, I did not touch people unless strictly necessary. I didn't even really hug my parents unless it was really required!).

And that was it... what I have come to learn of as a 'healing crisis' had started! That month I cried more than I had ever cried, I was not a crier... (the times I have mentioned in this book are probably the only ones I can remember for a very long time). I was a bottle it up and get on with it kind of girl with a smile on my face. Even during my depression, the only person who really knew was my husband. I had a bad temper and people often saw that, but they didn't see me cry, they didn't see me hurt but this month...I just couldn't keep it in as all the sorrow and pain that I had felt and seen over the years washed over me and had to get out of my body!

Field Note

We are all broken...that's how the light gets in! But first you have to let yourself break!

Chapter Eight - Ohhhhhhhhhh

This month, I mainly cried. Anything would set me off...a TV show, someone else being upset, the fact that it was raining...anything! And all of these memories kept coming back, the bad relationship I had had and how it wasn't all his fault although I had blamed him for years. The realisation that I had kept going back and I had let him treat me that way.

The baby I had aborted (although I had done this as I couldn't see another human put into the situation I was in...it wasn't fair to bring a baby into that!) but I felt guilty that I got pregnant in the first place...I knew how to not get pregnant! The decisions I had made to go into teaching, to stay in teaching, to ignore my instincts. The things that I had seen as a child (I never really thought they affected me that much but here I was crying over their memory). The guilt I felt for not seeing my nan when she was ill. All of these things kept coming to me...and they were making me sad...not in a depressed way but in a 'sad' way...I was feeling them.

And then the realisation that I had never dealt with any of these things. I had pushed them down and smiled through the pain. That was what had caused my bad back and my depression. I had never dealt with the pain of the things that had happened to me or taken responsibility for the decisions I had made in life. I had been a victim, I had blamed others for what had happened to me and I had felt guilty about things I had/had not done.

Then it dawned on me.... that's what had caused my ill health and my chronic pain. I was weighed down by the things I had held onto and my spine was being crushed. My hips were yelling at me to 'move forward' in life but I was stuck feeling like I had no power. My depression was caused by feeling like a victim and ignoring my part in my past.

And now I could see that I had ignored the things that were causing me pain because I didn't want to feel the pain. I didn't want to look at myself and admit that I had something to do with the issues that had happened in my life, that I felt guilty about decisions I had made. It was easier to push them down and pretend they weren't there, that they had happened TOO me rather than me being part of them. And the emotional pain I was feeling was coming out in my body...as chronic pain and depression.

And so, began my life of being honest with myself, of admitting that I had made choices that had led to certain things happening in my life that I hadn't liked. That I was not a victim of my life, others were not to blame for what had happened to me, I was part of it...all of it....the good, the bad and the ugly!

Field Note

To fully accept ourselves, what has happened to us in life, our mistakes and the role we have played in our own lives is how we break....and how we are mended again!

Chapter Nine - Seeing

By now Magic Mike had been coming down regularly to see and help my friends while I nagged him to teach me how to do it…. to which he always responded, 'When you are ready!'…which frustrated the hell out of me as I wanted to know now (and patience was not one of my virtues!). And then one fateful day he said 'OK' and pressed his thumb to my forehead. At which point I was like an inquisitive child opening just one eye to see what he was doing. And then he sent me on my way until next month!

And what a month that was! I had randomly heard about a meditation group that one of my friend's mums ran and started going along. There were two people in particular there that I felt I knew…although I couldn't place them, and I liked it because they talked about really interesting things like auras, and the universe, which I had never really thought about before but was getting very interested in!

I also had the feeling I was being followed ALL the time and could see someone out of the corner of my eye, stood in the doorway. The outline of a male figure resting against the door in my hallway…. which freaked me out totally!!

I went to one of the ladies from the mediation group (the one I felt I had known for ages, although actually I had only met her twice!) and explained what I kept feeling with tears rolling down my face (there I was again, crying in front of someone I hardly knew!). I was afraid...I hated all things supernatural, I couldn't watch ghost films or horror films and now I had this 'ghost' around me all the time. I didn't know what to do...what if it hurt me, or my family...what if it wanted to...I didn't even know what I thought it might do...but I couldn't stop noticing he was there!

It was a month of me being on edge and scared as I felt like I was in a ghost movie! And then Magic Mike came down and I said I kept feeling things. Quite blasé, he simply said 'that's OK, I'm just going to assign you another two angels to help you'. Angels what...I didn't even believe in angels and I was being assigned two more, and then it dawned on me...the man watching me, always being there, following me, was my guardian angel... (who I later found out was called Michael!). Another Michael to add to the list! So, I had spent all month being freaked out by ghosts and the supernatural when it was my guardian angel who had been with me!

Now at this point I was not spiritual at all....in fact I was quite humanist in my approach to life. I thought we were born, lived, died and went back to the earth with no thought about anything else really.... although I had always wondered what the point in all this was! Well, I was about to be enlightened!

Field Note

Sometimes things are not what they seem....
sometimes they are...and sometimes we need to
get past our own small minds and fears to see the
truth!

Chapter Ten - Questions

In a few short months my theories on life had been totally turned upside down. My hips, back and depression were pretty much fixed, (I still had a little bit of pain sometimes) in a freak meeting with a man I spent an hour with. I had not only one but THREE guardian angels, who apparently can be assigned to you by another human and my hands kept heating up for no apparent reason!

Life had gone from being pretty ordinary and a bit crappy to being really freaking interesting! I couldn't read enough about guardian angels and why they were here and what they were hear for. I had read so many books in the last two months (which was surprising as I always hating reading) but for some reason I just couldn't get enough information about anything and everything to do with life, the universe and all things a little bit strange!   However, I still hadn't figured out how Magic Mike fixed my hips and back. But I knew they had to be related...somehow!

By now you will have realised that I have a scientific background...and that's part of what I love to look at, how and why the body breaks and how to fix it. But western medical methods weren't giving me the answers I wanted anymore. There were too many gaps, to many unexplained phenomena....my hips and back for a start! And I still couldn't understand why my hands were heating up when I was around sick people. But more than that...I would get these odd twinges when I was around people, like a random pain in my knee or a sudden pain in my back as I passed someone in the street. I even felt teary around some people for no apparent reason.

And then I stumbled upon the term empath...an interesting phenomenon where people can actually 'feel' other people's pain.... usually in an emotional way (like when you start crying because your best friend is crying!) but it can also mean that you feel their physical pain....and that explained it! The random pains I would feel as I walked past people or stood near them, I was an empath! At this point I had started a side line business in remedial therapies as I now had the qualification, so I thought I should probably do something with it! And when I was massaging people I would feel 'hot spots' and everyone was commenting on how hot my hands were all the time! Time for a chat with Magic Mike!

'Why do my hands keep getting hot...and why do people have hot spots?'. Again, in a quite relaxed and 'Mike' way, 'It's because of inflammation, you are 'feeling' inflammation in their body, and your hands are hot because you are healing it!'.
Ummm.... not terms spoken of in western medicine! So, I decide to go on an alternative course for crystal healing to see what that was all about.

The lovely lady teaching the course was really nice and did a healing session with me...'you're not very grounded' she said, 'Let me help you with that'. And so, I get a treatment to 'ground' me. I have never felt so bad in my life...like I am literally walking through treacle.... this does not seem right to me at all! But I am grounded now for the next 24 hours until I go to sleep and wake up again feeling much better and less treacle like!

Another trip to see Magic Mike....'Why is grounding good....and why did it make me feel like wading through treacle....?. Again, very blasé and relaxed the response comes back... 'Because you are from a fairy realm, you're not supposed to be that grounded...just put your roots in the ground a little and float about two inches off the floor!'

Field Note

Sometimes the weird and wonderful really are weird and wonderful and the most random things make the most sense!

Chapter Eleven - Finding Me

Well, that was an eye opener! I always loved fairies as a child and had all the flower fairy books...and mum had just started to clear the cupboards at our family home and had given them all back to me that week! I started to look up realms and find out more and more about souls and what they were, and why we were here. I found out that fairies have an uncanny knack of throw 'anger bombs' at people...and realised I had been doing that my whole life! If people annoyed me I would throw them 'that look' as my mum said, and a huge argument would ensue...so I stopped doing that immediately and I had a lot less arguments!

Then I discovered the book 'Indigo Adults'...a very interesting read! By this point I was choosing books on the way they looked...I felt a bit like a magpie...if the book appealed to me visually it usually had something 'interesting' to say!

Now I always felt like I didn't quite 'fit in' here, the world was a bit of a funny place, I didn't really understand why I was here and what the purpose was although that had been buried a long way down. If you asked questions like that when I was younger you were seen as weird and there was no point so I stopped asking!

But Indigo Adults was a very interesting book, talking of people who don't feel like they fit in and how there were here to change the world and make it better...get rid of the wars and lack of respect for the environment! It was so true...this was how I felt... I didn't want to live in this world.... I wanted to live in a better one, but I had pushed it so far down to 'fit in' to life as I knew it that I almost forgot how I felt...until I read this book! Again, things started flooding back! That was it...I didn't really fit in because my view of the world seemed so different to other peoples.

Now, as an adult I had forgotten how to say what I thought, I had forgotten that I was my own person and I had been just 'following the crowd' as I didn't know what else to do!

Field note

Being the odd one out... the psychedelic Sheep of the family isn't always a bad thing.... learning to embrace it makes you feel so much better!

Chapter Twelve - Realisation

By now life was becoming a little 'different'…but definitely extraordinary! I was from a fairy realm, I could FEEL other people's pain and where they needed healing and I was a Crystal child, a soul that didn't quite fit in because I was here to make a difference to the world!

And then my daughter got sick…my amazing beautiful 4-year-old daughter got really sick really suddenly…on Christmas Eve 2016. We took her to the doctor on Christmas Day who sent us away saying 'she had a chest infection'. But I knew it was her appendix…. I don't know how but I just knew it was. By mid-afternoon Christmas day she was really ill, she wasn't interested in anything, she couldn't stand up, she was really poorly so we went back to the doctor who eventually (after tears and an argument) sent us to the ward.

Again, the doctor said she had a chest infection which I tried to argue because I knew it wasn't that. But doctors have a way of making you feel like you are wrong! An x ray later and the doctor said, 'No it wasn't a chest infection'. Her lungs were clear, she would have to get a surgeon to look at her. The surgeon said he thought it might be appendicitis although it wasn't presenting normally, and 4-year-olds didn't get appendicitis. She was too young to get operated on in that hospital, so we had to wait for an ambulance to come and take us to Bristol...a two-hour drive away, and an eight hour wait for an ambulance.

So, there we were on Christmas Day (well Boxing Day now) waiting for an ambulance and my darling girl took a turn for the worst. She was screaming and writhing in pain and I remembered what Magic Mike had told me, 'You can heal people'. So I did the only thing I could think of, I held my hands over her, but she was hot everywhere what could I do...? I asked for help from someone, anyone up in the sky...and it came to me...I had to flush her body with white light...so I visualised a torrent of white light coming from the sky and washing all her pain away. Within seconds she had fallen asleep and looked peaceful, without pain and I had remembered how to heal!

When we finally got to Bristol the amazing surgeons there took her to theatre to operate and came back to let us know she was OK...although it had been a very unusual surgery. Instead of exploding, her appendix had 'fallen off' which they had never seen before. And more than that the cord attaching it had completely healed (usually they have to sew it together so no stomach fluids leak). The surgeons and the nurses at the hospital were so baffled that they went in search of other cases like this and couldn't find any evidence of it ever having happened before in any medical journals anywhere!

So, although it can never be 'scientifically' proven I know in my heart that my torrent of light and inner knowing saved my daughter's life! FYI my little girl is fine now!

Field Note

Never discount your gut feelings they are usually correct! And just because it can't be explained by science doesn't mean it can't happen!

Chapter Thirteen - Remembering

After a very stressful Christmas and New Year life started to settle down a bit. Then I started to 'remember' things.... random things like being in World War one and being stabbed with a bayonet.... or hanging from the rafters from a barn (a vision I had had before when I was told how my grandad's brother died but thought nothing of).

I always loved the film Moulin Rouge and thought it was kind of glamourous to be to a courtesan (a very random thing to be drawn to really). And I had 'memories' of being one...a past life memory. These were all past life memories! Randomly, I remembered my pimp when I was a courtesan, he was the man I had had the very bad relationship with...the one I just couldn't seem to stay away from!

So, that was it...I did a course in Akashic records (the book of life for earth) so I could go look at past live properly rather than just having random memories of how I died. And something that I had never believed in 'past lives' became very real. Including the laws of karma and how we can bring past life issues into this life if they were not healed in the previous life!

At this point I had had a very strange conversation with one of my friends. I had read the story of how Hitler's mum had died and was very upset by the whole thing, like it was personal to me. Then I actually stuck up for Hitler...yes, the Hitler from world war Two! As the words were tumbling from my mouth I couldn't quite believe what I was saying but it was coming out anyway!

A little trip to the Akashic records was in order. I saw Hitler...Oh My God.... I was Hitler....! And.... deep breath...no I was looking at Hitler, so I can't have been him, but I did know him in a past life...quite well apparently! And then it came to me, the fact that I had watched his suffering as his mother died and watched what he had turned into and it felt heavy, in my chest, in my heart, in my throat and a familiar feeling swept over me of being powerless, of not being able to help, of watching something I could do nothing about. Many of the feelings I had felt as a child as I watch all the things go on around me but was too young, to innocent, too unheard to do anything to help. And the laws of Karma became all too real. I had watched helpless in previous lives and I had been watching helplessly in this life.

Field Note

Sometimes the reasons we are here and the things we go through are a mystery until we look... really look at our inner and outer world!

Chapter Fourteen - Piecing it Together

Not content with looking at these lives and what I had brought with me, I started to link other things in life together. My draw to Ancient Egyptian history, the papyrus of Rameses the Second with Horas that I just had to have, the orgonite pyramid I was so drawn to, and the cat which took my fancy that I couldn't leave at the breeders (I have now come to realise he is the incarnated soul of Nefertiti!). I went in search of why all these things made their way to me!

And I remembered...I was Isis (not the rebel kind!) Isis the Egyptian God who had a child Horas, who was the guide for Ramesses the second and his first wife Nefertiti. The Isis who brought her brother and husband back to life who incidentally (or not so much!) is also reincarnated in this time in the form of my now best friend (the girl whose hen do I went on and met Magic Mike!).

All of this also brought with it the very real realisation that I hate death, loss and suffering still to this day and always have. It was the reason I couldn't go and see my nan when she was ill and the reason I couldn't embrace being able to heal people (healing them means I see their suffering... quite a predicament!) I realised that this has been one of my life lessons for many lifetimes...dealing with loss.

Being able to see spirits now I realised I had a big que of them behind me! I spoke to a few of them and realised that I had held on to them lifetime after lifetime and that they were weighing me down! I have released all these souls now and sent them home. I feel lighter, more able to do what I came here to do!

I also realised that the reason I am a hear is because I hate to see people in pain or suffering and that I should use my voice and my skills to help those that are, rather than sitting quietly hoping everything will be ok!

Field Note

Sometimes the things and the situations around us give us the most clues.

Chapter Fifteen – Embracing Extraordinary

And so, I realised, embracing my extraordinary is how I can help and why I am here. Letting people know what we can do, all of us as humans if we choose to uncover our extraordinary, embrace our special gifts and share them with the world.

I started to see myself as the creator of my world, the one who could make things happen in my life instead of standing in the side lines watching and waiting for someone else to make a difference.

So, baby step by baby step I started to change things, the way I thought, the way I acted. I started to make life what I wanted it to be, to use my voice, my gifts and to follow my heart. And life became extraordinary!

Field Note

Life doesn't always turn out like you think it will…. sometimes it's much more extraordinary!

Field Notes

So, what have I learned during my journey from ordinary to extraordinary...?

That we are all extraordinary in our own way.

That our physical bodies can be healed but it's not always easy!

To see life as a gift.

To notice the clues around me and put the pieces together.

That our uniqueness, our gifts are needed in this world.

That we are powerful.

And that the world can change, one person, one action, one choice at a time.

Be the change you want to see in the world

Mahatma Gandhi

About the Author

Clare is the owner of Harmonize Healing, based in Devon, England. Clare combines her 20 years' experience of working with and studying the human body with her newly 'remembered' knowledge of healing to help those with chronic pain and illness to awaken to their true power and heal from the inside out.

Clare uses the Akashic records to see past life issues that may be affecting you in this life. Helping to clear trauma and karma allowing you to move forward in life.

Clare has designed a series of guided mediations to help awaken your inner knowing, clearing the way for you to experience your extraordinary!

You can find her at:
www.harmonizehealing.uk

Printed in Great Britain
by Amazon